Montessori & Music

WITHDRAWN

Montessori & Music

Rhythmic Activities for Young Children

Elise Braun Barnett

SCHOCKEN BOOKS · NEW YORK

INTRODUCTION

This collection of folk tunes and excerpts from pieces by well-known composers is designed for children from three to eight years old.

There is a saying, "In the beginning . . . was *rhythm,*" and it is rhythm that makes the first musical appeal to the child. Many educators, particularly those who were associated with Dr. Maria Montessori and with Emile Jaques-Dalcroze, base their music teaching on a belief in the primary importance of rhythm. Children do not listen in the so-called "grown-up manner," sitting quietly. They like to move with music. They express their feeling for the music with their whole body. If they are encouraged in this expression, they gain the inner satisfaction that comes from the union of their movement with music. The music becomes part of them, and this is, after all, the truest measure of appreciation.

Since the music that children hear forms the basis for their future musical development, it is of the utmost importance that they be exposed to the very best. It is with this idea in mind that the material for this book was chosen. The folk tunes were selected for their rhythmic qualities, spontaneity of expression, and simplicity. These qualities are closely allied with the things children like and feel. The same qualities are also found in the music

of our greatest composers. I have selected those compositions that lend themselves most readily to movement. The choices are, understandably, personal ones, and of course they do not exhaust the vast treasury of music.

Before discussing the music and suggesting ways of using it with children, it may be of interest to describe how this collection came about, and how the great Italian educator Maria Montessori came to play so crucial a part in the selection and presentation of the music.

In 1924 I was a member of the *Arbeitsgemeinschaft.* This working commune, in some respects similar to the American settlement house, was located in one of the worst slum areas of postwar Vienna. To it daily came children of working mothers; they spent a long day, often from 6 A.M. to 6 P.M., at the *Haus der Kinder,* a kind of daycare center, conducted along the same lines as the *Casa dei Bambini* which had been established by Dr. Montessori seventeen years earlier in Rome. Dr. Montessori took a lively interest in our work, and came to visit from time to time. On one of these visits, she found me at the piano, playing for the children. This was the beginning of an association that lasted until her death in 1952. She helped me develop the teaching of music along the lines of her principles of education, and, after I had myself taken one of the Montessori training courses, she invited me during subsequent courses to conduct sessions on the teaching of music in Rome, Milan, and London.

Dr. Montessori's genius was her absolute openness and attentiveness to whatever was before her, her ability to understand and analyze phenomena, and then to find ways to apply this understanding in her own creative way, with love for the child her guiding principle. It was this that led the first woman medical doctor in Italy to see in a psychiatric ward for retarded children the way for a new method of education for all children, a method which has since gained worldwide acceptance. Her philosophy of education was based on the fundamentals of human existence: living means growing and developing, and its manifestation is spontaneous activity. Children grow and learn when moving freely in an environment prepared for their benefit. She was the first educator to design an environment scaled to the child. It was furnished with light tables and chairs the child could move around, low washstands, and possibilities for "household" activities—plants and animals to be looked after. There was also ingenious didactic material designed to arouse interest and lead children toward finding solutions through self-motivated repeated use. Each material was designed to meet some specific need. There is no program, no set curriculum, but when— and only when—the child is ready and interested, he is invited to explore a particular piece of easily available apparatus, to use it as often and as long as he wishes, and so to master a skill meaningful to him at that moment.

Once the child begins to concentrate on an activity, the teacher does not interfere or interrupt. Montessori knew that the valid impulse to learning is self-motivation. The teacher is the custodian of the environment and the didactic material; she offers the child stimulation, but ultimately the child learns by himself and is motivated by the work itself.

Montessori introduced the joy of "doing-learning" at an early age. The didactic materials emphasize sensory-motor education; they are devised to develop the senses of touch, taste, smell, vision for the recognition of form and color, and acuteness of hearing. An example is the set of sound boxes, six paired cylindrical closed boxes that produce sounds of different intensity when shaken. The identical "sounds" are first matched; they can then be arranged sequentially from softest to loudest or loudest to softest.

One of Montessori's most important discoveries was the so-called sensitive periods. This refers to a special sensibility during the process of growth. It is a transient disposition and limited to the acquisition of a particular trait. Once this trait or characteristic has been acquired and absorbed, the special sensibility disappears, and any later learning requires much greater effort. Children between the ages of three and six are sensitive to sensory-motor activities, which provide foundations for subsequent intellectual development. With such background, the intellectual growth occurs earlier than usual and is greatly accelerated.

It is during these same early years that the sensitive period for singing falls. But the rendition of a heard melody can occur only after "understanding" through coordination of body movement and the music's movement—

the rhythm—is experienced. Hearing music, then, is the necessary preparation for making music, and therefore daily "concerts" are an integral part of the Montessori program.

The pieces in this volume are divided into different rhythms corresponding to various movements that children are able to perform. Experience has shown that there are three groups of movements embracing nine different rhythms. They are presented here in the order in which the child develops the muscular coordination to perform them.

1. Spontaneous movements: walking, running, galloping, and skipping. (The tempo of the music is adjusted to the children's speed.)

2. Adjusted spontaneous movements: trotting (slow running), slow walking, and slow marching. (The tempo of the children's movements is adjusted to the tempo of the music.)

3. Step patterns: a waltz step and a polka step.

In the first group (ages 3½ to 4 years), pieces using rhythms from Group 1 are suitable. Pieces for walking, running, and galloping can be introduced to this age group, but not those for skipping. Though skipping is a spontaneous movement, it cannot usually be performed with ease by children under five years.

In the second group (4-5 years), the child is able to adjust the tempo of his spontaneous movement to the tempo of the music he hears. Music for trotting and slow walking, as well as slow marching, can be introduced to him at this time.

When the child has more coordination,

he can try simple dance steps. It will now be easy for him to learn the steps of the waltz and the polka.

Music is best introduced during the morning. When children are still "working," but the teacher or adult feels that a "change of atmosphere" would be welcome, she clears part of the room, goes to the piano, and starts to play. Some children will interrupt whatever they are doing and joyfully move to the music; others, more cautious, will watch for a while before joining; others may just remain "hearers." There is no urging by anyone to join. Dr. Montessori's attitude to formal group-teaching was expressed most clearly one day: she attended a dancing class for small children and remarked, "This reminds me of canaries in a cage."

I have found the following plan of presenting the material to children to be very successful:

Walking and running as contrasting rhythms should be introduced together at the beginning. Only the first piece of a group should be used, until the children are able to move smoothly to that piece. Since most of the selections are short, and since children like repetition, it is advisable to play the pieces over several times without pause.

Once the children know their rhythms, they enjoy hearing a succession of pieces in different rhythms and tempi, and they react to them without any direction from the teacher. At the end of some of the rhythm groups, there are several selections with rhythmic changes, marked by ⊕. Youngsters usually like these very much.

Even though the children at first are interested mostly in the rhythm of the music, they later become aware of the melody and the musical character of each piece, and they will express this awareness in their movements. Every piece should therefore be played with all the details of phrasing, dynamics, and tempo.

Details of interpretation are given at the beginning of every rhythm group. Tempi are indicated by metronome markings. I have, as far as possible, adhered to the original tempo, dynamics, phrasing, and key that the composers have indicated for their pieces. A few pieces in each group are very easy to play. It is advisable to practice the more difficult ones before playing them for the children.

Some additional hints:

The piano should be placed so that the pianist can see the children.

The adult should not talk to the children while the music is being played.

Between pieces, necessary directions can be given with musical signals, such as:

Encourage singing and all other spontaneous expressions.

The music activity session should be planned to include about eight to twelve pieces. The program of each session should have pieces in contrasting moods, tempi, and rhythms (as in a symphony!). Children often help in programming by asking for their favorite selections.

A wonderful phenomenon occurred with children who for some time were exposed to the "concerts" contained in this book. They suddenly started to sing the music. While they had been seemingly reacting to the rhythm only, they had absorbed the melodies. It was almost a miracle to see that little children were able to sing more than one hundred "pieces" without having been taught.

This collection does not offer an all-around musical education for young children. However, it is an important factor in laying the foundations for the enjoyment of music. Much can be gained at this age through being part of the active participatory audience of these "concerts."

ACKNOWLEDGMENTS

I remember gratefully my teacher, the late Dr. Maria Montessori, under whose guidance this collection was made. My thanks go to all my colleagues in the *Haus der Kinder* in Vienna, especially Mr. Lawrence Benjamin. Grateful acknowledgment is made to the teachers and students in many countries who took Montessori courses, and who, during their musical training, suggested various pieces. May I express my appreciation particularly to my colleagues at the City College of New York, Professor William D. Gettel and Professor Jack Shapiro, for their musical advice. I would like also to mention the many children in my classes who asked for more and more music.

I also thank my daughter, Hedi Maria, who urged me to have these selections published because she believes she benefited from her childhood experiences with this type of musical training. I hope this collection will help more children to love music.

CONTENTS

WALTZ STEPS

POLKAS

Montessori & Music

MARCHES

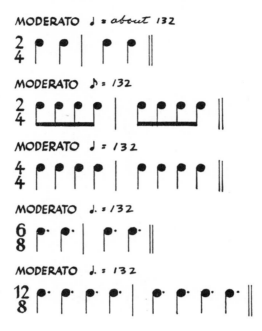

The tempi for marches are faster for small children than for older ones. Young children make quicker, smaller steps.

Play strongly and energetically.
Do not use too much pedal.

OLD FRENCH BUGLE CALL

MODERATO

SOLDIERS' MARCH

GAY AND DECISIVE

SCHUMANN
op. 68 No. 2

DUTCH FOLK TUNE

SERBIAN FOLK TUNE

HUNGARIAN FOLK TUNE

UKRAINIAN FOLK TUNE

FROM: "CARMEN"

BIZET

WELSH FOLK TUNE

JEWISH FOLK TUNE

GERMAN FOLK TUNE

ANDANTE

THEME IN 4th MOVEMENT
BEETHOVEN SEPTET, OP. 20

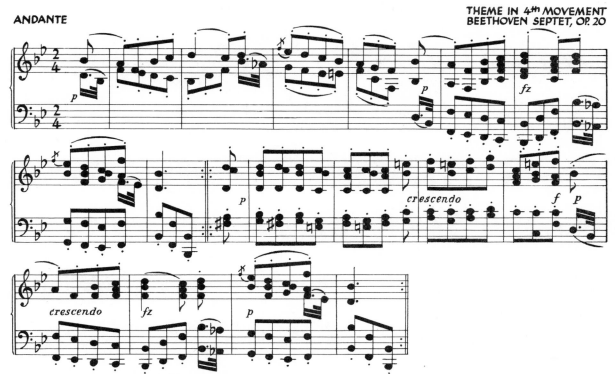

The staccato signs mean : Disconnect the notes, but give them their full time value.

WHEN JOHNNY COMES MARCHING HOME

MODERATO

PATRICK S. GILMORE

POLISH MARCH SONG

MODERATO

FRENCH FOLK TUNE

MODERATO

USED AS THEME
FOR VARIATIONS
SUITE #5
HANDEL

FRENCH FOLK TUNE

ARRANGED IN
"L'ARLESIENNE"
SUITE #2 BIZET

ALLEGRO DECISO

FROM "FAUST"

ALLEGRETTO DI MARCIA

GOUNOD

RUNS

ALLEGRO ♩ = *about 132* (*2 steps for every beat on the metronome*)

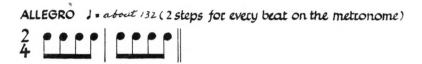

ALLEGRO ♩. = *about 80* (*3 steps for every beat on the metronome*)

Younger children take faster running steps than older ones, so adjust the tempo of the pieces to the speed of the movement.

Play lightly; use hardly any pedal.

The end of a phrase is indicated by '')."

RUSSIAN FOLK TUNE

ALLEGRO

GERMAN FOLK TUNE

ALLEGRO

RUSSIAN FOLK TUNE

ALLEGRO
CAN BE PLAYED ONE OCTAVE HIGHER

PUERTO RICAN FOLK TUNE

ALLEGRO

LITHUANIAN FOLK TUNE

ALLEGRO

second time piano

PILLOW DANCE

ALLEGRO   JOHANN STRAUSS, SENIOR

FROM:"ORPHEUS IN THE UNDERWORLD"

ALLEGRETTO MODERATO   OFFENBACH

CZECH FOLK TUNE

ALLEGRO

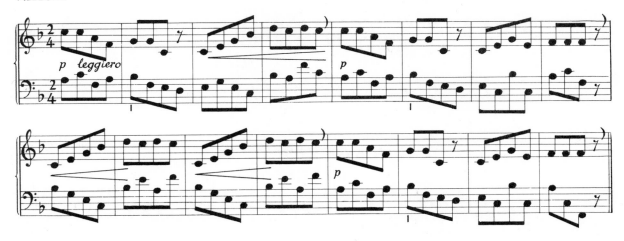

FROM "IN HUNGARIAN STYLE, LIKE A CAPRICCIO"

BEETHOVEN

Known as:
"THE RAGE OVER THE LOST PENNY"

SERBIAN FOLK TUNE

FROM QUARTET op. 74 #2

FROM: "L'ARLESIENNE" SUITE #2

ALLEGRO VIVO E DECISO

BIZET

DANISH FOLK TUNE

FROM: SONATA A MAJOR "ALLA TURCA"

MOZART
K. V. 331

FROM "AIDA"

PIÙ MOSSO

VERDI

ENGLISH FOLK TUNE

GERMAN FOLK TUNE

POLISH FOLK TUNE

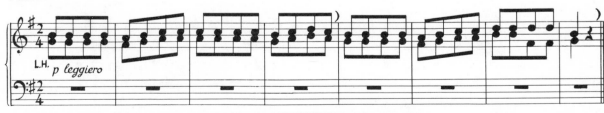

GALLOPS

VIVACE ♩ = about 120

2/4 [musical notation]

VIVACE ♩ = about 120

4/4 [musical notation]

VIVACE ♩ = about 120

3/4 [musical notation]

VIVACE ♪ = about 120

3/8 [musical notation]

The gallop movement consists of a step followed by a leap, or a step followed by a slide.

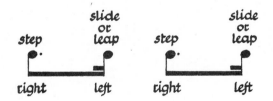

The gallop can be also done sideways, in which case it is always step — slide — step. The arms can be stretched out to the side.

Younger children do the movements faster than older ones, who take more time for a high leap.

Play with vigor, accent the beats on which the step is made. Use very little pedal. Play staccato, as though the fingers would be doing the gallop.

The end of phrases is indicated by ")."

VENEZUELIAN FOLK TUNE

VIVACE

STYRIAN FOLK TUNE

VIVACE

Left hand louder when repeated. (Note imitation.)

SPRING AIR

VIVACE

JOSEF STRAUSS

SCOTCH FOLK TUNE

IRISH FOLK TUNE

FROM "POLACCA BRILLANTE op. 72"

WEBER

GREEK FOLK TUNE

VIVACE

FROM "THE MASKED BALL"

ANDANTE MOSSO QUASI ALLEGRETTO

VERDI

FROM "TANCRED"

ALLEGRO

ROSSINI

FROM "THE PROPHET"

ALLEGRO CON SPIRITO

MEYERBEER

FROM VARIATIONS "LA CI DAREM LA MANO"
(MOZART)

ALLEGRETTO GIOCOSO

BEETHOVEN

FROM "FIDELIO"

ALLEGRO VIVACE

BEETHOVEN

FROM: SONATINA op.100

ALLEGRO

DVORAK

FROM: SONATA op.70

PRESTISSIMO

WEBER

SKIPS

ALLEGRO ♩. = *about 112*

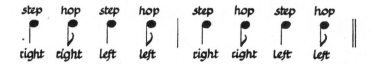

This movement consists of a step followed by a hop on the same foot.

step	hop	step	hop	step	hop	step	hop
right	right	left	left	right	right	left	left

As one foot does the hop, the other foot swings forward with the knee high.

Disconnect the notes in playing the pieces. Use little pedal.

The phrase marks are indicated by ")."

SWISS FOLK TUNE

ALLEGRO

DUTCH BUGLE CALL

ALLEGRO

ENGLISH FOLK TUNE

ALLEGRO

GERMAN FOLK TUNE

ALLEGRO

IRISH FOLK TUNE

ALLEGRO

DUTCH FOLK TUNE

ALLEGRO

NORWEGIAN FOLK TUNE

ALLEGRO

DANISH FOLK TUNE

ALLEGRO

ENGLISH FOLK TUNE

ALLEGRO

FROM "DIE FLEDERMAUS"

ALLEGRO MODERATO

JOHANN STRAUSS

34

GERMAN FOLK TUNE

ALLEGRO

USED IN 'PAPILLONS' SCHUMANN op. 2

HOP STEP HOP STEP HOP

SCOTCH FOLK TUNE

ALLEGRO

AMERICAN FOLK TUNE

ALLEGRO

OLD ENGLISH FOLK TUNE

ALLEGRO

GERMAN FOLK TUNE

GALLOP

ENGLISH WASSAIL SONG

VIVACE

TROTS

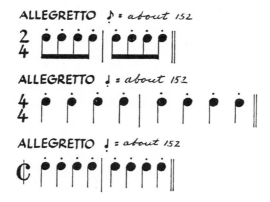

This movement is like a slow running step, except that the knees are lifted high. Variations of this movement have been invented by children:

Marionette Step

Legs and arms move stiffly, knees and elbows straight, the feet kick forward.

Jumping Jack

Legs and arms first astride and then together, jumping in place.

Tiptoe Step

Walk lightly on tiptoes.

Play very sharp staccato notes, as if the fingers were doing the trot.

Do not use any pedal.

As the children usually find this movement rather strenuous, avoid too many repeats.

Phrase marks indicated by ")."

GERMAN FOLK TUNE

ALLEGRETTO

SWISS FOLK TUNE

ALLEGRETTO

38

GERMAN FOLK TUNE

ALLEGRETTO

ECOSSAISE

ALLEGRETTO

SCHUBERT op 18A

FROM "IF I WERE KING"

ALLEGRETTO

ADAM

FROM SONATA op. 53

ALLEGRO MODERATO

SCHUBERT

FROM "MIGNON"

ALLEGRETTO

THOMAS

FROM: "THE MASKED BALL"

ALLEGRO

VERDI

FROM: TRIO op. 14 #1

ALLEGRETTO

MOZART

FROM "CZAR AND CARPENTER"

ALLEGRO

LORTZING

ITALIAN FOLK TUNE

ALLEGRETTO

FINNISH FOLK TUNE

ALLEGRETTO

42

FROM: QUINTET

ALLEGRETTO

MOZART K.V. 581

HUNGARIAN FOLK TUNE

ALLEGRETTO

MUSETTE

BACH

SLOW WALKS

Slow Walks

ADAGIO ♩. = about 52

As the children step on the dotted quarter note, they usually sway their arms and body from side to side. They often sit down and express the music with free body movements.

Play the pieces expressively, with singing touch, use pedal.

ITALIAN LULLABY

FRENCH LULLABY

ENGLISH LULLABY

AMERICAN LULLABY

THE LITTLE BOAT

MENDELSSOHN op.99#4

CATALONIAN FOLK TUNE

NEAPOLITAN FOLK TUNE

ADAGIO

FROM: SONATA A MAJOR

ANDANTE GRAZIOSO
MOZART K.V. 331

46

ADAGIO

BASQUE FOLK TUNE

ADAGIO

GERMAN LULLABY

ADAGIO

NEAPOLITAN CHRISTMAS CAROL

USED IN
"THE MESSIAH" – HANDEL

SLOW MARCHES

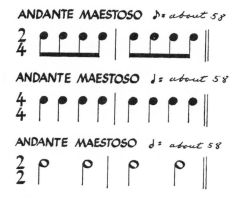

These pieces are more suitable for older children, who are able to feel the solemn mood of the music.

Play with sonority; use syncopated pedal on every beat.

NEAPOLITAN FOLK TUNE

FROM "CARO MIO BEN"
("THOU ALL MY BLISS")

POLISH FOLK TUNE

FROM "IPHIGENIE EN TAURIDE"

UN POCO LENTO

GLUCK

FROM: SONGS WITHOUT WORDS "FUNERAL MARCH"

ANDANTE MAESTOSO

MENDELSSOHN op. 62 #3

FROM "AIDA"

ALLEGRO MAESTOSO

VERDI

PRELUDE #20

LARGO

CHOPIN op. 28

FROM "AIDA"

ALLEGRO MAESTOSO

VERDI

FROM "QUINTET"

IN MODO D'UNA MARCIA
UN POCO LARGAMENTE

SCHUMANN
OP. 44

STEP STEP   STEP STEP   STEP STEP

WALTZ STEPS

The waltz step in forward direction (turns may be added later) is:

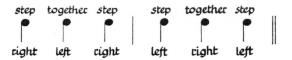

If younger children find this step difficult to learn **one** might try the "balance step" first.

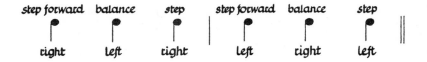

"Balance" on the second beat means: shift weight to the rear foot, while lifting the forward foot. On the third beat put the forward foot down again.

Play in a slower tempo for the balance step; otherwise, the tempo can be varied from the minimum to the maximum tempi indicated.

Play the melody with a legato singing touch and with expression.

Accent the accompaniment on the first beat. Use pedal, but not too much.

GERMAN FOLK TUNE

MODERATO

PORTUGUESE FOLK TUNE

MODERATO

SWISS FOLK TUNE

MODERATO

LITHUANIAN FOLK TUNE

MODERATO

52

POLISH FOLK TUNE

MODERATO

SPANISH DANCE

MODERATO

SWABIAN FOLK TUNE

MODERATO

CATALONIAN FOLK TUNE

MORAVIAN DANCE

AMERICAN COWBOY SONG

54

NORWEGIAN FOLK TUNE

SLOVENIAN FOLK TUNE

SWEDISH FOLK TUNE

GERMAN FOLK TUNE

CZECHOSLOVAKIAN FOLK TUNE

WELSH FOLK TUNE

CARINTHIAN FOLK TUNE

MODERATO

SLOVENIAN FOLK TUNE

MODERATO

POLKAS

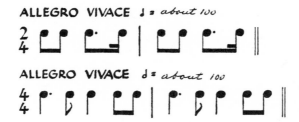

The polka step is a waltz step, followed by a hop.

Play the polka with energy and vigor; do not use too much pedal.

AMERICAN FOLK TUNE

ALLEGRO VIVACE

DANISH FOLK TUNE

ALLEGRO VIVACE

58

SWISS FOLK TUNE

ALLEGRO VIVACE

POLISH FOLK TUNE

ALLEGRO VIVACE

ENGLISH FOLK TUNE

ALLEGRO VIVACE

LITTLE BROWN JUG

ALLEGRO VIVACE

J. E. WINNER

HUNGARIAN DANCE

ALLEGRO VIVACE

FROM "DIE FLEDERMAUS"

TEMPO DI POLKA

JOHANN STRAUSS

FROM "THE MAGIC FLUTE"

ALLEGRO

MOZART

FROM "THE BARTERED BRIDE"

MODERATO

SMETANA

Less advanced players may play the last eight measures only.

FROM "MAMSELL ANGOT"

POLISH FOLK TUNE

ROUMANIAN FOLK TUNE

GRATZER GALLOP